Words for Empty and Words for Full

Published by the University of Pittsburgh Press, Pittsburgh, PA 15260

Copyright © 2010, Bob Hicok
Manufactured in the United States of America

Printed on acid-free paper

10 9 8 7 6 5 4 3 2 1

ISBN 13: 978-0-8229-6077-5

ISBN 10: 0-8229-6077-X

for Eve

CONTENTS

In these times

My sister's out of work and my brother's
out of work and my other brother's
out of work, these are facts available
over the phone or in person, just as now,
three clouds travel north, one
above another, smallish, amoeba shaped,
and the bottom cloud just died,
and the top two have joined forces
and left me to fend for myself
under a new sky.

How vague is that, amoeba shaped?
That could be anything: cigar shaped,
Manhattan shaped, could be libor, T-bill, jobs report,
which arrive as theoretical entities, words
from a teleprompter repeated by newscasters
and converted to waves beamed to satellites
and bounced to my set to be reconstituted
as their basset-hound eyes of concern
when the day's dollop or wallop of woe
is mashed and rehashed by people
making good scratch for telling us how bad it is.

There's little to hold in what they say.

That's what a job is: a pencil to hold, a scalpel,
shovel, "A Statistical Analysis
of the Probability That Anyone Will Read
the Statistical Analysis," even such slippage
is a mind-hold that keeps some someone
from drifting off into irrelevance.

I could offer this in Hegelian or Sartrean terms
of engagement before the void, but really,
if you're alive, and sentient,
you're an existentialist in that you know
most of what awaits is neither breath
or the electrochemical dream of you
you carry forth and mix with fellow soothsayers
of the eternal mysteries, know intuitively
that work is money, honey,
but also and maybe moreso, is your hands
kept busy with needle and thread, hammer and scythe,
memo and counter memo, is you
joining the thrum and hum that is all there is
except what there is not.

My sister's out of work and my brother's
out of work and my other brother's
out of work, these are facts known to many
and more many every day,
there but for the grace of a W-2
go you, as I'm employed by this poem
that's about to lay me off, I remember that
when the question of what to do
gets intellected about.

Jobs to do because there's work to do
because this whole to-do's
a stopgap measure to the zip
or heaven to come, about which
we haven't a clue.

A little Keynesing now or a lot of keening
later, when the phone rings
and maybe it's you whose house
is no longer your house, whose car's

just been slicked away by a guy
tatted-up all goth and penitentiary,
you whose kid needs grub, me
who has to mumble through
some version of

     could you, I don't know, maybe send me,
      I hate to ask, a few bucks?

If you never had to make that call,
let me kiss the inside of your skull, let me intercede
on the part of the burned field
for the grass,
on the side of the cadaver
for the walk under moonlight, I'm only praying
you listen to the theory
that how we get to be alone
is how we work to be together, since there are stars
inside your thumb, your breath,
and how you say *yes* or *no* is how they shine
or burn out.

After the procedure

All the apples have been washed.

I sprayed every apple with a liquid
that cleans pesticides away.
I prayed very leap myself with a quid

that kneels pesty vices away. On the counter,
pictures of my wife's stomach. Her esophagus
and duodenum. A-OK, her inner life, while she

sleeps drugs on the couch. While she
rugged peels no the slouch. The worm crawled in,
took pictures. Endoscopy. The sun comes in,

warms my eyes, drops bits of far away
against my looking. I am grateful; she fully great.
She will rise and be herself, a dash

inside out, invaded, but here and projected
in that state to remain. I am thinking soup.
I ma, thin king of do. Do make lunch, wash dishes,

do inspect her breath. It is there, the up and down.
I kiss her paper esophagus. Intimacy evolves.
Intimacy solves. I never expected love.

All the apples have been washed.

Some things that come together in coming apart

How stuck am I on the polar ice caps
now that they're not so much there as historical
novels people pretend to have read
but really, who has the time? Like it's haveable,
time, like we can stop driving ourselves
to the market and crazy soon enough
to have anything left to claim for England. Melting things
on that scale beats the yo-yo I stoved to goo
and a spanking, someone
needs to come along and send us to bed
without supper. In our defense
we're stupid, gullible, smelly, we're not
stupid, that was mean and categorical,
we're wired and emblazoned and impressed
by the singing of birds who are merely
shuttling air from one spot to another, holding it
as we do each other in a waltz
to let it go further on, where it must fend
for itself. These bits of song-air
and dance are changed forever, everything
is changed forever all the time, I'm not here,
I'm up ahead, running with my arms thrown back
to embrace how mild life seemed
when I first noticed light coming to rest
on my mother's face. Creatures
who generally have trouble with story problems
may not be the organisms one should ask
to anticipate global warming. A car
about to be started in Poughkeepsie
is the tipping point, after that, all is fire
and water, all is lost· do you
shoot the driver, learn the backstroke,

enjoy long walks into the high ground?
I keep returning to the ice caps,
their vast calvings in my mind, TV stars
of our dissolution, my head
thunderous and cold and too small
for their wounds but well-suited
to my hair. The debate as I understand it:
it's too late, it's not too late. Smart people
agree we're not that smart. Here are clouds again,
telling me they make this up as they go.
If we don't owe it to ourselves to fix
what we've broken, we owe it to ponies.
That was manipulative, but I love ponies,
how they let our children
ride them in circles with helmets on in case
the circles fall.

See side

Mind as wave: whoosh. As wet. As yet
thinking needs a dress to wear, what better look
than sea green or sea foam, within
never gets out without without, how cool
is that, that the sealed self's
not an option, hence the object of my affection's
conception. As in, I notice you
on your boogie board, therefore I exist
to see you're bad at balance, a savant
of oops. The fall's all we've perfected,
reaching for the apple with the words of our hands,
the yums, the Henny Pennys at our disposal.
I come onely, you two. Boo-hoo. Group hug, the all
of us, this wave charging hard, foaming
at the mouth, as if to slather with embrace.

Life

is so big. Eyelash in the salad. Aldebaran
        light-years to the right
                        of the margaritas.
Five hundred thousand
        new "jobless claims." Quotes. Was Bonaparte a fool
                        or a genius? Yes.
Rates of currency exchange, thermal exchange,
        chromosomal exchange. I begin
        to fill up, as if I'm a glass
and the world is water, is rain
                        is storm. Backfire
I think is gunfire and gunfire
                I'm sure is close.
The feeling that mysticism
        is the only way to be polite, that the stick
        fetches the dog. While I was masturbating,
                more rainforest
        disappeared. The feeling the sun is saying
do something.
        The feeling it's impossible
        to know what to do. So there I was:
planting bulbs
        for a greensudden spring,
                dialing my congresswoman, blushing,
        hanging up, redialing,
                        rededicating myself
to gestures, walking right up to the sky
                                and asking it please
                to stay.
        The slog
                the trudge,
                        pushing the boulder the pie-chart the petition

up the mountain. Save the whales,

the decibels,

the Earth,

the me. When I thought of life

as climbing the shadow of a tree,

I climbed.

When I thought of life

as a race between words

for empty and words for full,

I was at the end of this poem.

Scenic Thanatos

Dog
fucking a dog
while a third
dog watches
outside of
Famoso beside
almond trees, some

of these fields
have been used
so hard
fertilizer
has turned
to salt, I am

driving
to LA
where I've never
been to tell you
it is lovely
sometimes
how eager
we are
to die

BRCA1

She has the gene, the cytosine, adenine
her mother sister had, her sother
mister had, they've named the gene.

If I named a gene
I'd name it Gene, I knew a Gene,
brother to Greg.

We are like genetically
mice, tiny creatures with toes,
she is like genetically
87 percent likely
to have breast cancer, ovarian
cancer: ovum, Oppen, open, closed.

So come July, away with thee,
mammaries and ovaries, live together
in imperfect harmony . . .
it only takes a day to remove the real
and add, pick a word: prosthetic,
cosmetic, the faux breasts and the egg sacks
are just gone, call them the nothings,
the novaries.

And there I am/was
cringing, and there she is/was
smiling, touching my hand, saying nonononononono,
this is a good thing, the best thing
the universe has come up with
since the wet kiss, I am taking
dialogic license there

but she was happy as a torch
in a Frankenstein flick.

The townspeople have gathered
to kill the monster.

It's dark, but they have fire,
she has fire,
she's going to kill the monster
that killed her mother, her sister, if I may pare-a-phrase
down to its essentials:

hurray.

But ouch.

Hurray.

But seriously: ouch.

And the world, one day, had a second sky,
a sky for just the sky
to stare up and deepblue
and into, and a lake for the lake
to dive giggling in
and doggypaddle across, and a new
and soon improved her
sitting there mid-life
grinning brights, grinning hard-core
and full-bore and seriously
madcap happy about a knife.

Endangered species

Very busy sensing there's nothing down the train tracks except
remembering there are only five remaining speakers of Mohave.
There might be a loose and rusted spike, a smashed bottle of Bud
is likely if I walk long enough into picturing a basketball team of
old men and women in a gym in Oklahoma bouncing an orange
ball against a team made up of how the rest of the world can't
understand them. Coal trains come through here, taking across
the mountains what we've taken from the mountains, I think this
is like walking over cows while eating a burger, and feel filled up
on the empty feeling night is good at bringing to me like flowers
before a date. Here, night says, I brought you this bouquet of gone,
and it occurs to me these are the flowers of negation the man who
spent a night in a foxhole with a dead Viet Cong was handed over
and over. He doesn't talk about that, there's not a single speaker I
know of the language called "this is what it's like to dig a hole and
be alive in your death with the example of what that looks like."
Nor am I the last speaker of the language called "I will too often
use crows to express my deepest self," which it turns out is only
centimeters below the surface, now that we're trying to go metric.
The gravel sounds like breakfast cereal eaten straight from the box.
If night is crows touching wings somehow in place, stars their eyes
and the moon a hole in the patience of crows to obliterate, only the
air, with its high absorption rate for dead languages, could speak
of this to the past, which I've been trying my whole life to get in
touch with. So the last speaker of Mohave will soon be sitting on
the edge of her bed, noticing for a last time the beauty of cups, the
entirety of their existence the honor of holding and giving over,
emptying fullness into the empty mouth, and she will whisper a
word the cup has heard many times over, and when she's dead,
someone will take the cup away without putting it to their ear to
listen to the last, the entire ocean of what is left of a people. They
will be gone, the cup taken to a new life full of waiting for water to
come. I understand that sensation most of all, feeling there should

be something inside me there's not a word for in English or Urdu or Wichita. In grunt, perhaps, in the language I've called "heat this blade upon the stove and press it against your forearm," absolutely. If languages have to die, kill that one. Every time I walk it down these tracks and leave it, it drags its way back and kisses the neck of my sleep with its teeth.

A wedding night

A groom goes out with a pillow to where the sheep
are white bushes across the hill. Dirty white

bushes across the hill and places his pillow
at the top, just before the top, a few inches

from the top for his head so he can see, almost, yes,
he can see the curve of the earth, out

where there is only water. But there is a ship
on the only water, on the curve of water

to his left and right, as the dirty white bushes
move, as the ship moves to the east

along the curve, and he thinks of how his pillow
will smell in his bed, beside his bride,

of grass and sea salt and the curve of the earth
and coming home, she will breathe all of these

when she leans over him, drapes his face
with the night of her hair, the curve of her

falling to all sides, from a center, from a moon,
from an asking, from a giving, from now on.

Kinesis

The cutting board falls sideways
because of the cookie sheet behind it
and breaks the Krups carafe.
I go online thinking Krups
made munitions for Germany using Jews
to death to find they sell the carafe
for not much and order it,
hoping slave labor's not involved.
I make coffee with the press-pot
and notice that we're out of painkillers
for Sasha's hips, when they don't
actually kill the pain, do they,
just like I don't really love you
to death, I do actually love you
for putting the green bottle
of no more painkillers out
where I'd see it while I was thinking,
thanks to Krups, of tefillin, sacred words
on parchment in kosher leather boxes
strapped to the forehead is excellent
devotional weirdness in my book and how many
cups of coffee does this press-pot make?
Sasha limps more and more these days, as do I,
your ears are ringing off the hook, God
is calling to say He's not coming, a local kid
was killed yesterday in the war, shot
clean through the head. What's clean
about this? Dirty through, nasty through,
toothsome and biting through,
I've been working on the lexicon, all
the livelong day. While my coffee's
too hot to drink, the wind picks up
to tell me I better ask if you'd prefer

not buying anything by Krups, like you don't
want a Volkswagen, even though the new Bug's
cute, because of the six million
instances of ash you're a part of, like every drop
of water's a citizen of its cloud. We can do that,
cancel the order, stop drinking coffee,
use the Greek word "phylactery" instead
of tefillin, which I enjoy saying, phylactery,
it sounds like factory and prophylactic
put together, doesn't it seem
like every second, if you stop, has this whole life
inside it that is so completely yours,
it would die without you dying to never be
without it? I want to live to be three hundred
and sixty two. We should have
a new coffee pot by then that doesn't makes us
feel like we're waking to genocide, though we are
and good morning.

Punk, or a mouthful of sweat glands

—for Matt Siegel

All you need is a guitar!
Mine is red and salivates!
That band spent a million dollars on their hair!
We use Rust-Oleum on ours!
We'll never rust in the rain!
We're a cliff-dive of hormones and stage fright!
Sincerity should leave scars!
Our pose is more switchblade than your pose!
I miss when gods roamed among us!
Music is free!
Feedback is nourishing!
I have a plate of it every morning!
Twenty seven hundred bands played at The Anvil last night!
At the same time!
Blood clots because it's full of exclamation marks!
They slam together and form scabs!
Excitement keeps us alive!
Fuck the hegemony of chords!
You cannot borrow the safety pin through my nipple
to repair your drawers!
It's aerobic to subvert the symbols!
Let them fall!
Democracy should be amplified to fever!
I vote with my drums!
Anarchy means never having to say
"I will now read the minutes of the last meeting
of the subcommittee on housekeeping!"
You stole my tuneless screaming!
It takes three minutes for the avant-garde
to become fashion!
Punk is dead!
Long live whatever werewolfing comes next!

Something always comes next!
It's in the womb right now!
Put an ear to our mothers!
Wear them like headphones!
All you need is nerve!
There are millions of nerves in the body!
Every atom of you is a Stratocaster!
Let's drink beer and think up band names!
The Irish Loogeys!
Nuns of Syphilis!
Who seriously believes garages are for cars!
See how I ignore the rules of punctuation!
Poets all want to be musicians!
Musicians all want to be musicians!
So much for the classless society!
Rage is to Eros as cunnilingus is to essential!
No one wants to be dead who has tried it!
But everyone wants to try it!
Thus all the noise!
The soothing soothing noise!

Redoubling our efforts

And a double would be handy.
While I talked to Charlie yesterday
as he fixed the leak in the hot water heater,
my double could have gone to Charlie's house
and slapped his son, who wants to join the army,
infantry no less.

But I hear you, Noam Chomsky.
Violence as a means of ending violence is illogical.

Sometimes I think there are three of you, Mr. Chomsky,
or four, given how busy you are
saying and writing smart things, though my wife
has issues with the one of you
who doesn't believe in Israel, being Jewish herself
and trusting there are structures in the brain
that crave a homeland. I know you like the brain too
is why I'm comfortable getting into this
with whichever Noam Chomsky does the brain thinking,
probably Noam Chomsky One.

I'm not smart enough for Bob Hicok Two or Bob, The Sequel,
maybe I'm a prequel of myself, I sometimes sense
a presence running ahead of me, saying hurry up,
that there's a rocket over my head, a kind
of diacritical like the umlaut over the a
in doppelgänger, suggesting the way to pronounce my name
is really whoosh.

So Charlie's tooling away, he's got this crescent wrench
as big as Noam Chomsky's thigh, he's taken the nipple valve
off and found the leak, we're talking about the army
and then somehow the Klan, which he saw as a child,

they gathered on a highway east of here, hundreds of men
dressed like beds, and we're each of us saying
the country might have stepped over the line
into fascism, and I'm thinking, I could send my double ahead
to the future to find out, to warn them, and stay here
and eat my double's share of ice cream and enjoy
his share of investigating the topography of my wife,
and Charlie fixes the leak and leaves and the cats
come out of hiding, and I'm walking by a mirror and noticing
the guy walking by the other side of the mirror, and I stop
and he looks at me like I bet it's better in your world
and I look at him like I bet it's better in your world.

So we're tied, you see, the two of us, when it occurs to me
that either one or both or all of us should be driving
to Noam Chomsky's house with enough pencils and paper
to work this all out, the why do we kill each other stuff
and the where does language come from stuff.

The only answer I want when the night taps me on the shoulder
and asks, did you try, is yes, yes sir, hard and double hard
and harder still.

This, that needs to be done

Woods the dirt take to the full bucket
of the? Woods they not. More of the blistered
shovel. More of the hours of bend to the bucket
of take. Lower now, how the Earth sits
upon itself, this smell of perhaps birth
the closer one to death. A hole has asides.
Bucket of woods, body sun up and sun down.
You: mover and moved. Woods the full of dirt
to take. Now less than was. You've made a hole
has insides. You have insides. You are a whole
other system of what might be done. Shore up
the adores: staves of water, lattice of prayer flags,
the wind doting on devotion. Cement the pour.
Stock the blocks. Come sun, come moon, this
take, this eat of dirt to the woods, the bucket
full of you are doing, how perfectly you fit
the glove of these minutes. No "as if," no "like."
Is. The is of filling your life with your life.
How good the tired of feels feels. Then sleep.
Then rise and again. Until some done is done.
There you are, with neither ladder in or out.
So you make that, but first the tools that will,
first the bend of your hands to the shape
of the tools. To hold. The hold a request
to be held by the fit of simply one thing
to another, you one among.

Keeping track

One grackle two grackles in the maple three four
two grackles one grackle in the maple none grackles
in the maple: I do ask them something
by looking at them, as they ask me nothing
by not looking at me, what is sky to birds,
four grackles in the maple and this sense of sky
in my head. As soon as five six seven eight
arrive, four hops to a different branch,
then a shuttling in and out like our subwaying
to work, now one, now none grackles, I am poor.
Then it is later and still none grackles,
still alone, though behind me, where I can't see,
some tweet, chirp, what am I, a xylophone?
I translate best I can, now a gaggle of, a swarm of
six, who knows for sure what singings
they really are? I don't, my ornithology's weak,
and while confessing my poor birding, six left,
the air favors minus slightly more than plus,
though I can look the air in the eye
and hold what is to what was. Was grackles,
was some need I had to feel
mending going on, without knowing
what's skewed or rent, now a crow
making the tree resemble an excuse for crow,
as I am an excuse for death to take its time.

Man to man

Thirteen killed by a man in Germany
and then himself.

Ten killed by a man in Alabama
and then himself.

I have killed no one, I am behind.

Are they out there
and we just don't hear them, stories
of men who go crazy
and mow the lawns of strangers?

What was he like, the interviewer would ask
a neighbor.

Kind of quiet, she would say.
You know: kept to himself.
A nice man, really.
And then he was just like, you know, mowing.
Mowing and mowing and mowing
and mowing. There were grass clippings
everywhere. It was horrible.

A man kills his girlfriend and then himself.

A man dresses as Santa, kills his family
and then himself.

On that day, I stood under a tree.

My standing under the tree
moved a crow from that tree to a tree
across the road.

When that crow moved, a second crow
and a third crow followed,
and I thought, I have moved the crows,
and thought, when I followed, the crows
have moved me.

I have done this a year now, gone from tree
to tree by crow, shooting no one as I go.

A man paints his wife green and then himself.

A man scolds the tulips and apologizes
to the roses.

A man gathers all the men in the world
and asks why rock paper scissors
won't do, why rock paper scissors
fire won't do, why rock paper scissors fire
atom bomb won't do.

The sound of all men shrugging
sounds like the sound of all crows
taking off from all trees, like the day
flying away from itself.

A man kills the day and then himself.

A man kills the sun and then himself.

I am telling you, Alpha Centauri, man to star:
　　　　　　　run.

A trinity of goods

O hush: o how? I hear of peace
but hearing flees, I rush to be infinities
at once. To run and word and fuck, to hold,
to rain: *'splain, Lucy,* Ricky said: I can't.
I'm not self-contained but self-maimed, self-
stuck. To change, I womb pebbles
under tongue, not the stuttering many
but imaginary ones. Of quiet, of ease,
in the theory pretend becomes mend,
the actor the part. An art: evolution.
I am yet a font of frail and false, of starts:
stuck. A bit of jittery sit, of mumbling om,
as I seek a sense of being
that has nothing to do with doing,
done. Good grief: good god: good luck.

Watchful

A wasp had built a nest outside the backdoor.
Every time I went to knock it down, the wasp
was working the chambers. I waited two days,
finally turned off the water
while doing dishes, picked up a knife,
went out and cut the nest free
of the doorframe, where it hung by little more
than a thread of wood the wasp had chewed
to pulp. The wasp was there, flew off,
and was back, on the fallen nest, just now,
when I checked after typing "working the chambers."
It started to walk away, the morning
too cold for flight, when I knelt
to pick up the nest. In each of the open chambers,
a grayish dot that will become a larva,
then a pupa, then a wasp who builds nests
for grayish dots. Two of the chambers were sealed.
I moved the nest to the top of a plastic box
enclosing telephone wires on the side of the house—
brightly colored wires with white stripes
running their length, wires of the human voice—
scooped the wasp onto a long, rusted hinge
that has sat for months on the porch railing,
placed the wasp on the nest, and came back to tell you
this is the poem I've been trying to write
about the man I stood beside during the national anthem
at a ballgame, who placed his prosthetic hand
over his heart, looking more like a boy from the outside,
where I was, and sang, in his uniform, harder
than I ever have, without a sense
of irony. Though how he would do that,
or what the inflections of irony are, I don't know,
or if it was two hands—a prosthetic, a phantom,

a grip, a ghost—over his heart, a memory
of his hand, his life, our country
as it was, whole, possible. I've wondered
every day since, like when the wasp was there, just now,
as if nothing had changed, when everything had changed.

Thinking of his hand as a phantom, just as the reasons
for the war in Iraq are phantoms. His hand a flame
as the burning of a Humvee is a torch. The sense
that we should not, who haven't been there, speak of nails,
bullets flying. Of war itself, this severing
itself. A piece of shop window, even a rib
blown free, ripping through the séance of his flesh,
the mood of his flesh to know and to hold. That
I should not, who has not been there, speak of this. But you see
how I start to. That a space is opened by his hand, absence
creating absence, and I have to fill it, it's what I do—
this isn't an *ars poetica*—it's what *we* do,
all we do, essentially, that dogs do not,
butterflies do not: see a thing and draw it
to another thing, make them clash and kiss, knit, gather.
His brain too is doing this. Fusing. Making
a kind of metaphor of sensation. His face, when he smiles,
when a breeze strokes, triggers the life of his hand,
for these encodings dwell beside each other in the cortex—
what the hand feels, what the face feels. And since his hand
is gone, and no sensations arrive to this region,
to this love, his face is taking it over, telling his mind,
This equals this.

Probably. Truth is I don't know. We didn't speak,
the man and I, of the ballgame, the weather, his hand.
Crack of the bat, blue sky, hotdogs
that smell at the ballpark like they smell
nowhere else. Perhaps he feels no haunting,
no ghost reaching for the butter knife, no itch

that isn't there being there, persistent as air.
Perhaps he would be Shiva for this war, acquire
more limbs to "lose" or "give," horrible words
that suggest misplaced keys or wrapped boxes
under tinseled trees. In an earlier version of this poem,
I used his hand as an excuse to write

   This equals this: I'm a phantom of the body politic
if I don't speak, I'm required to, freedom's
a tended dream, a public mapping of belief.
When we're silent, government flows into the spaces
we leave open, and remaps, acquires for itself
the severed faculties of democracy.

An excuse, a catalyst, an image to carry these ideas.
But I kept coming back to what I didn't know, what
I couldn't say, honestly, unless I made a character
of the man, and today, finally, on the ninth attempt,
it occurred to me that the absence of his hand
speaks of his absence from my life and my absence
from his. I know no soldiers. I know no one who knows
a soldier. So this is a war on tv, a program, a dream,
The Odyssey, The Green Berets, Platoon. Proximity is required
to feel, understand. I know the wasp, have looked into . . .
its face? its life? . . . have entered some moment with it—
crack of the bat, blue sky—existed with it in time, as time,
as do beings who act in sight of each other, giving life
the motion by which it exists, as trees are required
for a copse, an edge for deer to cross between the field
and safety.
   His hand, possible ghost reaching
for his wife's breast, for the cloth to draw
across his son's back in the tub, under which
his lungs rise and fall, rose and fell, with which he felt, feels,
his son's lungs, now, with his other hand. A severing
by class? Mostly. By money? Mostly. I know no soldiers,

So I know

He put moisturizer on the morning he shot
thirty-three people. That stands out. The desire
to be soft. I could tell the guy from NPR
that's what I want, to be soft, or the guy
from the *LA Times*, or the guy from CNN who says
we should chat. Such a casual word, "chat."
I'm chatting to myself now. You did not
do enough, I write to myself, about the kid
who turned in writing about killing
a few buildings from where he killed.
With soft hands in Norris Hall killed.
This is my confession. And legs I think
the roommate said, moisturizer in the shower,
I don't know what I could have done
something. Something more than talk to someone
who talked to someone, a food chain of language
leading to this language of "no words" we have now.
Maybe we exist as language and when someone dies
they are unworded. Maybe I should have shot the kid
and then myself given the math. 2 < 33.
I was good at math. Numbers are polite, carefree
if you ask the random-number generators.
Mom, I don't mean the killing above.
It's something I write like "I put my arms
around the moon." Maybe sorry's the only sound
to offer pointlessly and at random
to each other forever, not because of what it means
but because it means we're trying to mean,
I am trying to mean more than I did
when I started writing this poem, too soon
people will say, so what. This is what I do.
If I don't do this I have no face and if I do this
I have an apple for a face or something vital

almost going forward is the direction I am headed.
Come with me from being over here to being over there,
from this second to that second. What countries
they are, the seconds, what rooms of people
being alive in them and then dead in them.
The clocks of flowers rise, it's April
and yellow and these seconds are an autopsy
of this word,

                    suddenly.

Whimper

Don't know why the kid didn't come after me,
I nearly failed him, fail means differently now,
or some other English prof, also dead
is not in our mouths as it was in the past,
we'd have said dead about the place,
now that the semester's over and smiled
that we have a few months of grass and air
to ourselves, do know why I tried

to get him to talk, to have breath take the shapes
that excite our brain, that seem almost
to be a pencil or the kaleidoscope
with its insane colors I twirl in the window
to make the sun feel better the next time
it says, *I have nothing to wear,* I wear knowing
certain things are certain, that years from now

I'll be a man who buys grapes for the reason
anyone buys grapes, and in the way anyone buys grapes,
by eating some and putting some in a bag to be eaten
at a later date, with the difference that,
as I turn for a twist-tie if it's a store
that still provides them, not all stores do
and fewer I suspect will be so thoughtful
in the future, somewhere in that turning
I'll sense a parent some states away
dropping to the floor as I imagined
a moment ago, with no image of the face and the body
really just a cloud, it's the action
that's distinct, the cause, the erasure
of the daughter or son who went off to college
to get maybe a little drunk—the parents knew that—

a little laid, a little while passes and the picture
that's not exactly a picture passes too
and then it's back and this is just how things work
around here now, I'm a theater of these short films
of people I don't know falling down and being broken, why
do we think answers will help, and why ask that why

of the larger why, *why did this happen,* and why from that why
branch to the why am I alive why, there's the why
are we here why and the why do we let so many questions
begin with a bang why and the why do we say aftermath
when it never ends, the desire to add for some and subtract
for others, we say we want answers, that it's very quiet
around here now, all this light, the sun more full of itself
by the day until July will strip us of shadows and time
will seem to have given up on night, why is the song
we add to nature, we're like birds as kids, why why why,
we sang, we sing, whole flocks of us swirling now,
turning our turns into turning, not knowing
in our direction what our direction is, how things
get decided undecided, lost if you need to find us
is where we are.

Mute

Silence stood out. So nothing
took a shape in my mind, as of what:
        wind? The wave inside the wave
you don't see, what gives it shape and drive,
        what isn't but carries
flesh? For sixteen weeks
he didn't talk. I think I'm breaking the law

in telling you this but the Internet
        already knows, his un-
saying has been said, over and over,
through days and nights
        of teleyammer. A semester
of neither "hey" or "hello," not a giggle
over the stupid shit, no sigh
        for spring's tulips rising up,
just a shadow under the awning of his cap.
So to hear the recorded and resurrected him

ravaging with his rave, sputtering on
about his kinship to Jesus, his mad conviction
that we made him trigger a hundred rounds,
is to realize he lived tongueless
        in me, the circuits
that work the tentacles of speech, how we reach out
on air, into the nothing between us
        with the something,
the anything of talk . . . I didn't feel,
until I heard his voice, that he was human.
        We say this to each other

now, who knew him, how it was nearly
an out-of-body experience

to hear him speak. He's still taking us
out of ourselves,
            first breath, now our sense
that we had pegged the world. I often thought
of the energy, the oomph it took
            to remain mute,
to actively draw in the nothing
that we long to occupy
with song and chatter, the vacancy
            we seek to fill,
and let it fill him, let nothing
become what he was saying, a speech of null
and void. "Let there be light"

            is how we see the word,
and in that phrase is the code for language=
sight. Even now, I go back and listen
to what he was saying by not saying, I look
at my memory of that unsounding
for some kind of wisp, a breath,
            a gasp
I can examine for what it holds,
but there's nothing, no knob of sound,
            no uttered rung
to hang onto, and no letting go.

Troubled times

Each shot three times at least, thrice
we don't say much, I just now remember
I was trying to write that morning

about a goose being chased
in the field by cows, it suggests,
I remember just now I don't want to feel

what it suggests, I've been here,
at this point of failure, about to picture him
in the hall, in a room, and refusing

that presence in my life, though I can't go back
to the goose, the phalanx of udders,
I think I was writing "the cows lean forward

like cannon," refusing to water
the images, let them grow, it suggests
diligence, this is not a meditation,

they were funny, tons of waddle
chasing feathers, I don't want his face
behind my eyes, it's too easy to let him be

how I see the sun, I left a blank space
behind me a moment ago, I had to go back
and write "diligence" where nothing was,

nor will I strike a line across the word
to suggest my doubt, I'll just come right out
and admit my imperfections, that I am adrift

right here, in needing to talk about
but not wanting to glorify him, the parents
have lost everything, I've lost

something, I don't know what, it suggests
_____, now I'll leave blanks, will be
pointless, as if moo could trap honk,

my thoughts want to be bucolic,
they have these "pick your own" places
around here for apples and grief

I imagine grows from the brain seeing itself
one day in a shop window as it passes,
so many problems because we know we exist,

let us not know we exist, let us be blank,
three times each, I keep starting to see him,
an arm, a shoe, don't think of the blue unicorn,

the pink elephant, I can never remember
how that goes, the chartreuse aardvark,
how to unmind what's in mind, how to mine,

use, remove, to hold, so much to hold,
I bend to pick up the memo and the cockroaches
in my arms go free, disgusting, what I know now,

what do I know now, the goose got away, I am here
but here isn't here, the sky worn by the hours
like a cap that fits some other head

And on the seventh day, as if someone said,
"May the healing from the refrain
'May the healing begin' begin," we have Frisbees,
exuberant grass and thighs
against spring air, the sound
of sanding wood in breathing hard
not far from Norris Hall with suddenly
a fence around it. "Life goes on" is also painful

to hear, to see in truth that we have to get back
to wondering if eight of us can fit in the car
and where's the goddamned pizza with three meats
for $11.95? How do we not get down on our knees
and pray every second to the machine? Gears of trees
and tulip cogs, such a churning mixture of air and sex
and pizza fueling the device, keeping the chug-a-lug
going full-speed, full-bore, full-tilt, listen
to all the phrases with full in them. Students are full

of being full of grief, it's coming out their feet
as they sprint after the Frisbee,
as they track down freedom and set it loose
again and again. Catch and release, the end and birth of joy
in the grab, stop, pirouette, flick of a kid
who watches the others dash off and turns
toward the memory of the shots, I see him
not knowing how to look in that direction
in his own way, which is distinctive
from my stupefaction—perhaps a bee
in his left ventricle versus the piranhas
in my brain—and then he's back
and doing this pointless thing
with his whole body like every lunatic

In the loop

I heard from people after the shootings. People
I knew well or barely or not at all. Largely
the same message: how horrible it was, how little
there was to say about how horrible it was.
People wrote, called, mostly e-mailed
to say, there's nothing to say. Eventually
I answered these messages: there's nothing
to say back except of course there's nothing
to say, thank you for your willingness to say it.
Because this was about nothing. A boy who felt
that he was nothing, who erased and entered
that erasure, and guns that are good for nothing,
and talk of guns that is good for nothing,
and spring that is good for flowers, and Jesus
for some, and scotch for others, and "and"
for me in this poem, "and" that is good
for sewing the minutes together, which otherwise
go about going away, bereft of us and us
of them, like a scarf left on a train
and nothing like a scarf left on a train,
like the train, empty of everything but a scarf,
and still it opens its doors at every stop,
because this is what a train does,
this is what a man does with his hand on a lever,
because otherwise why the lever, why the hand,
and then it was over, and then it had just begun.

Shorn

Morning. The usual crows. The usual undulating line
of Paris mountain coming out of the dark or into light,
take your pick. I'm writing about the shootings again.
I don't mean to. I don't mean to write
about writing again, but the mind, shorn of object—
object of the poem, object of the bullet—doesn't exist.
It's the choice of object I wonder how people make,
why some words are enough in how they almost
don't fail, why some minds, like all minds,
are never seen, but their invisibility requires
the extension of invisibility, the extinction of the day
as it would be. With me in or out of it, this day
will be itself. I want to be in it, Cho
wanted to be so deep in time
that we can never get him out. This is what
I'm saying: I don't know what I'm saying. I'm saying
the hero cop was smart, determined, pretty
on TV last night. She and her men
went after a sniper, a boy
who'd shot several people from the roof
of a mall, circles of blood on their chests, backs,
reminding me of daubs of paint, pointillist deaths,
maybe. We were never told if they lived
or died, the people were props, he was stopped,
the boy, after she—still smart, determined,
pretty—said, "shoot the bag," meaning the bag
of pipe-bombs at his feet, and they did, and he exploded.
"Columbine" was mentioned but not Virginia Tech.
We were happy about that, brushed our teeth,
went to bed. Morning. The usual wondering
how one thing signifies another, where is the pure instance
of mind, of me, of crow, going on about,
what is it that crows go on about? I had it

Hope is a thing with feathers that smacks into a window

—for Gregory Hines

More bird strike.
More buds on the hours soon to open into waving.
We were driving seventy yesterday
for the sake of our hair,
so it could tug on our faces
and feel part of the tapestry or whatever throw rug
boring people say life is like.
We are boring people who thrust our arms
out of cars in the belief that flying
will notice and come to wrap us in the lift-off.
More childish behavior.
More *Diagnostic and Statistical Manuals*
to feed the fires we light of our neuroses
so we can see each other across distances
of not giving a damn.
I love birds and regret my house is a weapon
somehow concealed to them in the pants of the air.
We were doing algebra then each other then cocaine
then aerobics broke out like acne
upon our thin souls and my point is
we need a better phrase than shit happens.
Elegance happens and also tap-dancing
no matter how much we ignore it
won't go away.
For the foreseeable future, this is the sentence
of reminding each other it could be worse,
we could kiss like tacks, the horizon
could every night take one baby step backward
until wonder is erased.
All this stuff we don't need.
Punching each other in the head we don't need,

venerating the cadavers, this fear of transparency.
"Please look inside me" is followed by "please go away."
More time. More bird-song and wind-driving
and metal plates on our shoes
sounding like the telegraph's back in business
and it's good news. What is that,
good news?

To find the new world

There was a woman in the restaurant, ordinary in dimension and use of her fork, nothing sexually evocative about the procedures of sustenance as she practiced them, and I with good company, movie/book/art people, no great, out-to-sea lulls in the wording of the night, she seemingly also quite happy with the gab and grub, smiles essentially the menu. But at some point her forehead announced itself as a startlingly wide plane. I wondered why I hadn't noticed it before, perhaps while deciding between the rice and beef this-and-that or as one of the hes at my table said one of the things about the temerity of public discourse that was said, as if any of us are out there, tickling doorbells, asking mothers if they see what's become of freedom. What has become of freedom? All week I'd been feeling the abandonment of my body by my hips, which seem suddenly filled with rust, there's grumbling at work like sheared gears turning, and on TV, President Smirk telling me again that my life is none of my business. And there it was, this vast, slightly arching, almond-brown pause at the top of her looking, this space of no purpose other than to finish her face, to take her countenance where it needed to go, to her hair, which turned around and went the other way, touched her shoulders with its ten thousand strands of midnight and fell across her back, as if her body were a loop. Briefly I felt the responsibility to rise and kiss her forehead, that if I did not, that was the end of it, the forests would burn us down and toxins ooze into our sex and money realize it doesn't need us now that it has computers to play with. I didn't, didn't drop my napkin into some resemblance of an iris, didn't cross the room carpeted with dull versions of rose, didn't bring my lips to her skin as softly as tulips rest against the moon, didn't, didn't. So blame the Apocalypse on me, on my cowardice, my unwillingness to trust what I knew, that she'd have felt cool as a glass of ice water an hour after the ice has melted, and the water's reached over the top, to find the new world, to go about its business of going, and it would have been the start of helping each other, would have begun a dance across the restaurant, everyone seeking some small patch of skin, some truth they'd come to believe, and we would have all said yes to the dessert tray, yes we did save room, yes coffee, yes we'll come again, yes we'll have a nice night, yes there is no dearer child than yes.

Meditation on a false spring

I'd kill

        to be as hopeful as the weather, seventy-three
on February third, winter
         suddenly eager for the beach. It's natural
to love this, shirtsleeves and skin, the eave-ice
      of just a week ago
         · gone, as pole-ice
   melts into the generosity of ocean, into the vast
wave and salt you could taste if you kissed
           my lips, my blood.

                      Natural
because who feels
        the broken Earth? I feel
     sunlight, a breeze on skin and by the touch
         of looking, a breeze in the spasms of an oak's
zombie leaves, dead
           but hanging on. Who feels
carbon load? Change
         in albedo? A rise in sea level
in Galveston
       and decides, I will shoot my car? We feel

        happy and hungry and horny and other things
that begin with h, small
         and stupid and guilty, tired
and afraid and pleased, we feel
           what's near and intimate:
              not
"seventy-three degrees"
          but how sexual the touching air is
      without parkas. Small

things. Like when I found
                    a minute-hand in gravel
            when I was nine and walking
                    nowhere, and kept it
without sorrow for the watch, not just
                    without sorrow but knowing
            it took a death
                    for me to have this treasure, this "hand"
in my hand, pointing timelessly
                    in my pocket for weeks
                        until it was washed
            away in the wash: this
                            is how the mind works, is this
                    how the mind works: locally,
            on a scale
of pleasure? I keep

                    coming back to this
            in the context of violence—thirty-three
                    shot here, hundreds
of thousands in Iraq, billions since ever—how the one
                    meets and fits or doesn't
into the many, the single mind
                    melds or grinds against the ur-
            mind, I've tried to write my way
to understanding on a computer
                    that connects to a grid, and that grid
to a grid, and that grid
                        to systems no one
human can think, let alone feel, to fit my mind
                            to that disembodied mind,
            to the vast wish and oops and intelligence
                    and war that is the all
of which I am part
                    and example. Get

real: not going to happen. So how
hope or why
        hope, what is
            hope, I want
hope. Seventy-three degrees and I'll go running
        and think while running, I am the sensual beneficiary
of carnage, I am the last man who will romp
           through these woods wearing factories
on my feet, who ate
               a factory for breakfast,
        who has a factory at the end of everything
he touches, I will believe that, I believe
            that, and that recycling
is comedy, that turning off the lights
        is like wearing a pillow over my chest
to battle, how

        hope, I have hope, somehow
hope. Maybe it's just bloodbreathrhythm, the physical
           optimism of the heart, sys-
and diastole, maybe it's that I haven't
      shot myself
        in the fucking head yet, as we
              have almost
        not. Maybe hope's
      what I've long thought, a choice, a decision
I have to make as often
            as my heart decides
yes, until my heart decides
      no, and I mean
the actual heart, the actual world, the actual
        gun I touch to ask myself
    to prove this is a day
      I want in on.

Between us

—for BN

X is pregnant and wants to keep it
but can't, but can, but can't. I should put *it*
in quotes but that causes more problems
than solves. I'm not the father,
if you're wondering. And she's young
but not crazy young, not overcome
by the moment, first time, back of the car,
isn't beer wonderful young. So I think
she wanted to get pregnant, since condoms exist,
and convenience stores with their shelves
for condoms, and either she could've bought them
or he could've, together they could've engaged
in prophylactic foreplay. This is certainly not
an articulated desire, as it wasn't for me
and my girlfriend twenty-five years ago,
when there were also condoms and we didn't use them,
also diaphragms. I never could have said to her
that it was exciting to screw unwrapped,
to feel the possibility of a child in rut,
I barely recognized a wish that ran deep
as protein chains, as lung and sinew.
But when she got pregnant, the desire
to not have the child was stronger,
I should have been rip-sawed by my contradictions.
The maple outside my writing window's
coming into leaf, it's bud-sprinkled still
but they're opening, they're not recognizable
yet as leaves but palpably broadening
and insistent. My girlfriend got pregnant
twice and I learned the extent to which
I'm no more sophisticated than this tree—one

abortion, one miscarriage—the extent to which
the me I think of as me—word & memory me,
love of rivers, tapioca, Tom Waits me—shadows
wave me, thrust me, blood me, and what
thrust me wants, what blood me needs
is more, to make more, to extend, persist.
The cock will trick us, the womb seduce us
into serving the only reason they exist.
This woman is Catholic and wants to be a mother.
Anything she does now will be wrong,
from her perspective: there's no clear
choice, no right choice. The child
is not wanted, is not a child
but a fetus, the fetus is wanted
but not now. The fetus is not a child,
is not a dream, though she dreams of rain
in her womb. The pill is not one pill
but two pills, the child is not a child
but a fetus, is not wanted now, is wanted later,
when it will be a different fetus
not a child and then a child. She dreams
of bones in her underwear drawer, fingers
and jaw. She dreams of hyacinth
flowing from the tap into cupped hands.
She calls the father and says,
what were we thinking? She calls the father
and says nothing, breath on the line. I remember
holding my girlfriend's hand as she was made
a woman no longer pregnant, as the jar
was taken away by a nurse
whose shoes squeaked. I thought of basketball,
ten pairs of squeaking shoes,
which made me think of horse, a game my girlfriend
and I liked to play, which made me think
of the roan she and I petted that summer

a history of origami

two women in three days
      cried on the green bench in the park
          where i found a dollar
          folded into a boat.

i thought it was the crying bench and cried
      on the crying bench
          when it became available.

                  i cried
by thinking of all the people
      who've never broken a shop window, not the baker's
window, the bead-seller's,
      who sells beads for purposes
i find hard to list: necklaces,
the hanging of strings of beads
      in doorways, the owning of beads
          just in case.

breaking a shop window with a piece of shale
      the size of my heart, a piece of shale
          on which i've drawn my heart, not my actual heart
          but my feelings of my heart,
             since i've never seen my heart,
      would set something free.

i don't know what that something is
      but it would be free.

and my heart would have survived its travels
      through glass, its jagged voyage
      through my reflection.

you see now why i cried: none of this is real.

until i can answer "yes" to the cop who asks, is this your heart
among the ruins of your reflection?
i won't be a man, despite what my anatomy
insists.

it insists
that i overcome a sense of resistance when i move,
that i move
as long as i am able to move, and when i am unable
to move, that i stop.

it would be free and look like a bird, an actual bird
or a dollar folded into a bird, a dollar bird
in a dollar boat.

which is to say
i believe origami arrives
when we need it most.

i can't prove this but i can't prove
you're a good person though i suspect
you're a good person.

you who opened the door.

you who tipped your hat.

you who ran into the fire and carried
the fire safely out.

Minutes of the minutes

Was I trying not to step on the moonshadows
of trees? I think so, because of a gnosis
I felt in them, perhaps an awareness
of the sky, that they knew they owed their life
to its life, and tiptoed awhile. Noticed cows
curled in darker mounds of night in the field
to my left, then thought of this guy
I hadn't in years, a vet—stethoscope,

not M16—who wrote a poem called "First
of a Thousand Rectals," in which we learn
that reaching in to the shoulder and feeling
for the life going one of two ways, milk or meat,
is the only sure way to know if a cow
is pregnant, a funny and sad poem
about what it takes to understand. Horrible,

I admit, to place this image next to you,
but there you both were, inside my walking,
the you of talking earlier in the day
about a problem that refuses words, I could see
in your face how lithe this X is, this X
I won't tell, when you threw language at it
and I threw language at your language, it's all
we have, the basket we carry the world in,
but it feels so often like that poem, a blunt

reaching in. Do you ever wonder
about the last thing you'll do, the thing
you won't get to think about, go over and over
until it's worn to a shine or spent, how good
that would feel or if it would feel good, a gift

or an amputation? I noticed then how far
Orion moved without asking me, telling me,
and turned for Cassiopeia, which is almost
what I know of heaven: that it's hushed
and I'm not in it.

In the future, the future will be the past

A woman screamed
during the protest between supporters
of Arabs on one side and Israelis
on the other that Jews should "go back
to the ovens." There's a picture of her
on the Web in a white scarf, mouth open, everything
slightly blurry because she was moving
or the camera was or the Earth jumped a bit
at what she said. As I looked at the picture,
Eve was behind me folding a shirt, sleeves first
and then in half and then in half again
the other way, making me glad
I'm not a shirt, she coughed and I saw her
in an oven. This wasn't a thought
but a vision, not a Jew in an oven
but this Jew in an oven, not this Jew
in an oven but these lips, eyes, this voice
made ash. I got up and kissed her
to make sure she was there, not telling her
she'd just died in my brain,
then sat before the screen and stared
and stared again at the picture
of the woman, refreshing my gaze
at whatever rate humans do
who want to know what it feels like
to wear a particular head, to own
a different tongue. Sure that, if I could meet her,
if the crowd dispersed, if screaming
were put aside, if she sat across a table
from Eve and saw her stirring coffee,
worrying a hair into place, and I gave this woman
paper and pencil and told her, I am a god,

you can sketch anything you want to happen
and it will happen, she wouldn't sketch an oven
and Eve in the oven, wouldn't draw fire
but a hill, as all children draw hills,
as all adults are children in the universe
in which I am a god, a hill with a view
of other wavings from other hills—
these are examples of the thoughts
I have of people, as these are examples of questions
I ask the falling snow: if I could burn a sock
could I burn a foot, if a foot a finger, if a finger
an ear, if an ear a womb, could I ever burn
a womb, snow, in your opinion,
how did we get here?

Getting in line

A man crosses a field. He'd like something
to set down so he picks up a rock
about the size of a baby. Rock-baby
is heavier than a baby-baby would be,
the man has walked but a few steps
when he abandons the child. Years later,
there's a knock on his door in the field:
rock-baby has grown up and wants
to get even. The man
doesn't remember rock-baby,
so when rock-baby says, you never loved me,
the man says, sure, I can buy that,
and offers grown-up rock-baby a beer.
When they're a little drunk, the man says,
your quarrel isn't with me, your quarrel's
with the poet who put us in the field,
and the poet's quarrel
is with the God who makes poets
send people walking across fields,
and God's quarrel is with the nothing
that came before God
that God is always trying to fill, even after God
has filled it. Grown-up rock-baby
thinks the man is telling him
he doesn't really exist, he stones the man
to death to prove that his nonexistence
is not the case. Alone
with the bloody certainty
of his tangibility, he writes out,
again and again, "my thoughts
have a city in them." And in that city,
at night, a little girl
wants a goldfish for the goldfish

she already has, and the goldfish
wants a little girl for the little girl
he already has, and the bowl
wants a bowl beside it
to share the orange and rippling feeling
it would call soul if the word
wasn't already taken.

Learning to swim

At forty-eight, to be given water,
which is most of the world, given life
in water, which is most of me, given ease,

which is most of what I lack, here, where walls
don't part to my hands, is to be born
as of three weeks ago. Taking nothing

from you, mother, or you, sky, or you,
mountain, that you wouldn't take
if offered by the sea, any sea, or river,

any river, or the pool, beside which
a woman sits who would save me
if I needed saving, in a red suit, like flame

is the color of emergency, as I do,
need saving, from solid things,
most of all, their dissolve.

From the history of grade school

The pie chart's the only dessert-related
presentation tool I can think of, there's no éclair graph
or Jujubes overhead, which seems strange, even sad,
though were I to piechart this sadness
versus other sadnesses, allowing that I'm allowed
to create verbs whenever I want, it would look like this:

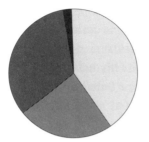

☐ SADNESS FROM
DRIVING OVER
WORMS AFTER RAIN

■ SADNESS OF THE
DARK SKY QUESTION

■ SADNESS THAT
LANGUAGE HAS A
MOUTH BUT NO EARS

■ SADNESS DUE TO THE
SWEET SOLITUDE OF
PIE CHARTS

It's a relatively thin slice of sadness, I'll admit that,
a diet slice, if you will, more of a sliver, honestly,
like when I was seven and dreamed
after a day of woods that a tree grew
from the sliver in my hand.
Imagine how I felt when I woke
and wasn't a tree, I was a boy, an average boy
no one would climb or hang a tire from
or cut a heart into to contain the names
of love. Here is the pie chart of that morning:

■ SADNESS THAT A
BOY IS NOT A
WOMB IN WHICH
A SLIVER
BECOMES A
TREE

That's 100 percent for you
who looked the other way during math,

out the window at the swing
ticking in the wind, at the swing
trying hard to do without you
what it did when you were together,
at the swing and the rust song you knew it sang
while the teacher went on and on
about your need to know certain things
to have what she called "a future,"
which is where you are now, in a future
discussed far to the right of the swing
you ran to as soon as you could,
past four-square and tetherball, past everything
that wasn't flying, wasn't you
flying, is how we all knew you'd lead us one day
out of the fires.

you are here

i was eating a sandwich next to the rape
of the sabine women and telling my wife exam
suggests my prostate will be asked
to name rivers and capitals when a cop
nodded to the no eating sign and i stood
and bowed to say in the body's esperanto
"i'm sorry" and he bowed too and turned
the beautiful wing of his italian nose and walked
where savanarola had been hung and burned
i believe both i believe i slipped my hand
under eve's shirt as we counted how many statues
were missing an arm a soul in the loggia lanzi (see
map below) then i leaned over and kissed her spine
once per vertebra up to her bra and rose
and we walked passed the uffizi in the dark
where david's tall and cracking and naked and bored
to the arno and didn't jump in because it's filthy
and we're sane and hadn't been to the boboli gardens
yet where a metal head four times as tall as me
maybe and wide suggested the scale of relativity
perhaps or the brilliance of gandhi thinking "just
don't do anything" and the british gave up
on oppression and a black cat circled my leg
as i was feeling the time had come to live
as if i am wanted

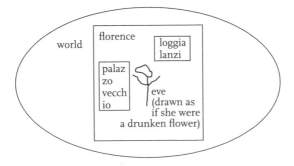

Foreign dispatch

   Paris is happy with America and I am happy
with Paris.

   With the Giacometti head in the Pompidou
that's largely a nose, almost the lying Pinocchio on a string
nodding subtly to the vibrations of the building, to the spin
of the Earth, nodding quietly I am sure
in the air in the box keeping it safe from people
like me, who would kiss today with equally bronze
or actual lips.

   The temptation to touch.

   To treat art as a prolonged embrace.

   Flying buttresses holding up the sky, the twelve arches
of the Pont Neuf, mothers pushing babies in strollers,
the prow of our genetic ship, through the Jardin du Luxembourg,
which exists because the Louvre bored a Medici.

   Walking and walking, a newspaper in my bag
with the headline, "Historique," walking and pressing my palms
to Marie Curie's tomb on the day a black man's
elected president in the States, walking and wanting
to make large statements about democracy, walking
and fearing large statements about democracy, preferring
a baguette, the egalitarian smell of piss along the Seine,
until it's dark and dancers twirl up and down
the art nouveau staircase of the Grand Palais
to the humping thump of bass for a video.

   I look in on a world that isn't mine and think
of exclusion—typically sexy Parisian thoughts—

that there's less of it now, more ways in, more places
to enter, more cities to stroll with a sense of charm, down
the Seine and across the Pont de la Concorde
to the Assemblée Nationale, where, as if on cue,
the Declaration of Independence is projected across the facade,
along with other documents of freedom, in anticipation
of the anniversary *de la Déclaration universelle des droits*
de l'Homme, and I read with a greater sense of dream,
of proof, how Americans want to see ourselves, how we ask
to be, until the words are gone and I wonder if any of this
happened—the election, the day's impossible alliance
of connections—and head back to the hotel, feeling tired
and that we're not who I thought we were,
as the Eiffel Tower's swept by a grand mal seizure
of light, twenty thousand flickering bulbs
going ape-shit as they do every evening, not just
when life as we know it has changed.

For the time capsule

Banks were given billions of dollars.
You'll want to know this, I'm writing it down
so you can read a poet's history of money
for the sake of charm or delight.
Hundreds of billions of dollars,
which if Christ started spending
at a million a day when he was a kid
and presumably broke, when he was a kid
and his allowance ran out,
he'd still be at it, still be baubling
his way down Rodeo Drive, Our Savior
of Stigmata & Bling. At the same time,
homeowners were losing their homes, loans
called ARMs had "readjusted,"
meaning the interest rates of the loans
went up: whole subdivisions
turned to kindling, whole families
became those people you drive by
when you take a wrong turn
on the way to the Ice Capades, who surround barrels
of fire downtown and you think,
how homey, how soon
can we get back to the freeway?
They were not, these fire-barrel people,
given money, they were not
because it sends the wrong message,
because a contract is a contract,
because in America, we lift ourselves up
by our bootstraps, which is impossible,
have you tried? You can lift one leg at a time
and hop or just stand there
with your lone lifted leg
looking like a great blue heron

or an OK blue heron
and call it progress, I wouldn't stop you
but I'd probably film you,
probably show people the film
and say, *what is he doing here,*
what was she thinking, I'd go to academics
and ask them to explain
the mythological and sociological
ramifications of the boot question,
even though I don't wear boots. The bankers
were not scolded to levitate by means
of magical footwear, and the gifts given them
were not called welfare, and the rules
governing how they spent these gifts
were nonexistent, and they were not forced
to shake a cup and plead, *sir, can you spare*
seven hundred billion dollars?
I tell you this to prove
we were a good people, a feeling people,
a people who didn't pick on bankers,
whose politicians applied the spiritual belief
that what you do to the least of us
you can get away with, I write this
for the day you look back and think,
no one can make this shit up, on a day
I hope to be overcome by the lyric,
"try a little tenderness," since songs
are just scatterings and bones without us
and we are merely screamers
without song.

Basic physics

They've discovered one hundred thousand
western lowland gorillas
as hummingbirds rejoice over sugar-water, as oil
comes off its high. Sing with me:

one hundred thousand western lowland gorillas
in the Republic of Congo, one hundred thousand
western lowland gorillas in the Republic of Congo,
shoot one down, chop off its head
for a trophy, ninety-nine thousand nine hundred
and ninety-nine western lowland gorillas
in the Republic of Congo.

That's the problem
with adapting a drinking song
to the human tendency to destroy: it doesn't scan,
though it's the loudest song
our consciousness sings. The song
of doing nothing is much quieter, in fact
no one's actually heard it, it's the Atlantis
of arias. Lately I've been drinking
a petite shiraz from California, I'm not sure
what's petite about it, tonight
I raised a glass to the idea
of an undiscovered world
inside this world, shielded
by something like the sunglasses
cops wear to look badass. I keep coming back
to Heisenberg, the impossibility
of leaving the observed
pure; I would like to be an animal
again, changing neither velocity
or direction. Like I said: lately

Now that the cow case is solved, I'm going to ask my cop chums to arrest the Nestlé Corporation.

> —can you describe them?
> —they make yummy chocolate, they deplete aquifers.

Imagine putting a corporation in a squad car.

Imagine going to the tap and nothing coming out.

Imagine being 70 percent sand.

I can't remember from my church days what makes holy water holy.

Probably that it is water.

First do no harm

While trying to extract a fly from a spiderweb,
I pulled one of its legs off.

There is the thought of small prosthetics, image
of a tiny hospital, tiny being too big a word
for the nano-this and micro-that, calipers
and scalpels and whats-its.

Once I grant soul, it's hard to stop.

Does a carrot have any, and if any, more than cucumber
but less than squash?

Philosophy should lead to salad.

I was trying to help. By this phrase
we have watch fob, atomic bomb, the Red Cross, how often
does anyone believe otherwise, does anyone say,
I was trying to muck things up?

A limping fly.
Were I a Hindu, I'd say it was or will be me.

I like that as the name of a river: Wasorwillbe.

The Wasorwillbe flooded, hundreds were killed.
Six months later,
the best crop of wheat in a century.

I see a boat, a man asleep in the boat, his hand asleep
on the water, a fly asleep on his hand.

A shopkeeper's story

I sell one bristle brushes. People
seeking two bristle brushes I send
to the guy on Amsterdam, who's in a rush.

I may have one customer a year
for my one bristle brushes, a one-eyed
lover of tanagers, she may have

one dollar to spend in the moment
light's neither day's or night's,
but one's where infinity begins. Whoever

she is, she's always painting barbules,
I'm always thinking, no one will notice
that they notice this, that her tanagers

move, that everything's alive. We talk
care and feeding of the one
bristle brushes. Care exists. I thrive.

One interpretation of your silence

Probably I hurt your aesthetic feelings.
How I said a thing, how I held a lamp
to the night. These should walk without us—
words, the dark—is perhaps your view
of existence. I can't know,

you provide no puppet theater,
no tumbling routine for me to engage
in spirited discourse. That a face
comes with every body, and a body
with every name, makes it seem

like we're the same species,
when a cursory kissing shows how multiform
any one puckerer is. I'm sorry
I'm not the Wednesday or club sandwich
you expected, imagine my surprise

that you're not the world peace
I really do want, it's not just a thing
I say to the judges inspecting my cleavage.
If you'll try again I'll try again,
how trying we are. "To the puppies" is a phrase

I carry around in search of the context
in which shouting it will change everything.
If you have no such rip cord, we really
shouldn't be seen together in public,
for you are the matter for which I am

the antimatter, and as *Lost in Space*
showed us if it showed us nothing else,

it's not good for life when they meet,
and I want to do what is good for life,
because I want life to return the favor.

Go _____

How exuberant the rally cap is.

Do you know the rally cap?

The rally cap is a baseball cap turned inside out
and placed on your head when your team is losing.

The idea is that change, any change, might presto a change
in your team.

So you look silly and it earns a home run.

So you lean one hand against the other and frame your voice
between the rafters of stars.

Prayer and the rally cap presume ears, the listening of God
or atomic structures.

You must do something, anything.

Say it's the ninth inning and you're down a passel of runs.

Say planes have flown into buildings and killed
how tall they were.

Say a storm has washed the color of a city away.

How do we ask the morning into our rooms?

Should we drop a fist into every conversation?

Does your bombing, sir, scold the catastrophes?

I love the rally cap.

It is the strangest verb I've ever seen on the head, a language
of please.

You must do something, anything.

Say you're being chased by a train.
All you have to throw at the train is your breath.
You would throw your breath at the train, your embrace.
Flying breath and embraces
would fill this world of rabid locomotion.
It would do no good
unless the train is afraid of this complicated air.
It would do no good
unless you have an explosive embrace, a breath
that can speak to the train and ask it, why are you chasing him?

A grenade embrace, a reasonable breath are rare.

Yet you'd throw them because everything changes the world.

Waking up does, the cardigan did, and these flowers of stitching
among the crowd, the simple turning of the inside
to the outside, this willingness to become a symbol
of want, of desire for a thing: I admire this use of flesh.

There is an end, and how we get to the end is all that matters.

You must do something, anything.

Say it is possible that I hate you.

Say it is possible that I love you.

Say that we're going to vanish and we know we're going to vanish
but we haven't vanished yet and we know we haven't vanished yet.

What this leaves is time—another inning, a near-infinity
of generations, of fucking things up
and fucking toward knowing more than we know now.

How to advance the runner without swinging the bat.

How to suture the wound with our lips.

How to take the scraps of touching the sky and touch the sky again.

The universe doesn't know we exist.

So we tell it.

Connect

I'm alone on my porch which is alone
on the mountain which is alone in the sky.
All this aloneness should be good

for something, an increase in telepathy,
the balancing of weight on the Earth
to keep wobble out of its spin. The clouds too
are solitary, have spread like students
into an empty classroom. The farthest,

which has evolved from a purple mustache
above the open mouth of the diurnal moon
to pink lipstick on the horizon
kissing the day goodbye, reminds me

of the guy in the last row on the left
listening to the professor in secret,
with his shoulders more than his ears,
who tips his desk back as a disguise
for his mind leaning in. I only know
enough about that guy to be that guy,

about separateness to be afraid
of a lecture on atoms, of the day I learned
that zippers and turnovers and even bones
are mostly distance. In the hall after,

I kissed a woman over her chest-hugged books,
one on art and another anthropology,
she loved beauty and that some people
gather in huts and some in offices
and some in churches but everywhere
we tend to huddle and rub. It occurs to me

I could have been comforted
by the book, by six hundred pages
trying to point out that we are prone
to make a whole, I should have known
as we kissed that some of my electrons

were in her and some of hers in me,
that atomically, everything's having sex
and where I end I don't. I come out here
to watch things be themselves
even though I touch them with stranger
identities—pine trees that I see
as the hair of the mountain, cows I follow
to know how a chess game would look

from above if the only rules were wander
and eat—I come out here to get better
at being alone but I get better at thinking
the slow gyres of vultures are how buttons
get sewn to the sky, that the wind
has a tune in mind when it touches the chimes.

Epithalamium

A bee in the field. The house on the mountain
reveals itself to have been there through summer.
It's not a bee but a horse eating frosted grass
in the yawn light. Secrets, the anguish of smoke
above the chimney as it shreds what it's learned
of fire. The horse has moved, it's not a horse
but a woman doing the stations of the cross
with a dead baby in her arms. The anguish of the house
as it reveals smoke to the mountain. A woman
eating cold grass in Your name, shredding herself
like fire. The woman has stopped, it's not a woman
but smoke on its knees keeping secrets in what it reveals.
The everything has moved, it's not everything
but a shredding of the anguish of names. The marriage
of light: particle to wave. Do you take? I do.

Do you too always feel differently the same?

For two days I've been saying, that's just the way I roll.
Try things on is a good philosophy, and look outside yourself
is advice that smells of lilac in the morning.
I would experiment with a tractor for my heart if I could,
the blood plowing, the rooting around for love.
It's embarrassing, though.
            Are you sure you don't want the medium fries for a penny more?
                 That's just the way I roll.
            Why don't you crawl off and die?
                 That's just the way I roll.
Daddio was before my time, I was born
into far out, psychedelic, man, but the vernacular
rejected my tongue, cool was as hip as I got
but everyone says cool, our grandmothers, Caesar, I can hear Manson,
it was cool, how they begged for their lives.
Revolutionary, such tiny changes
as using the red cup for coffee, as sleeping sideways
on the bed, then there's sharing,
noticing all the chicken noodle soup I have,
then there's not swatting the fly
because any killing's the beginning of all killing,
but when I open the door to let it out, two more come in.
Like nature or God, whatever, is saying,
that's just the way I roll, fuckboy, and so I've named them.
That one's Ellen and that's Kaisha and the one
flying upside down is Frank O'Hara, who I warn, when he lands
on the lampshade, beware the dune buggy ride.
Do you know flies fly backward?
It's tragic, that out of the billions there've been,
not one fly with its sesame seed brain
has ever thought, cool, I'm flying backward,
maybe next I'll fly inside out until I'm pretty

as a bee.
We don't get to know what we don't know, like right now,
every other direction this poem could have gone
is lost to me, like this, "the orioles are saying
copasetic," or this, "the night was a cliché of crickets
and humping,"
I know that dirge, I am that applause, the grinding,
the slapping of thighs against ecstasy, and a Mobius strip
begins life as a flat piece of paper, a line,
but add a twist, a bit of glue, and we have no idea
where beginning ends or ending begins, and maybe
they don't.

People who live in stones should cast glass houses

Could it be the modern art museum
in Chicago is a response
to paranoia? So much glass
and light, such an equality
between inside and outside, seer
and seen, an openness
to being open. I like to feel

and call it thinking, to think
and call it breeze: it's a sense, is all,
that we've been for years
a twitchy people, a trigger-finger
twitchy people, a torturously, water-boarding,
twitchy people. And that, whereas some
want you to twitch more, want you to eat war
for breakfast, others
want you to walk among DeKooning
in sunlight. Not far

from DeKooning in sunlight is Lake Michigan
in sunlight, where I've run
in sunlight and wondered
if a house built of spangling waves,
of water's embrace of the dive,
water's tolerance of shape, is the true
American architecture or the lost
American architecture. My head

as bathysphere only knows
to rise, knows the need
for breathe, for bright, and there I was
in Chicago, the sun
casting my shadow on pigments

of mind. And I wanted to tell someone
that this brush, this meld,
this collide, this sex
between boundaries is democracy,
so I'm telling you.

A primer

I remember Michigan fondly as the place I go
to be in Michigan. The right hand of America
waving from maps or the left
pressing into clay a mold to take home
from kindergarten to Mother. I lived in Michigan
forty-three years. The state bird
is a chained factory gate. The state flower
is Lake Superior, which sounds egotistical
though it is merely cold and deep as truth.
A Midwesterner can use the word "truth,"
can sincerely use the word "sincere."
In truth the Midwest is not mid or west.
When I go back to Michigan I drive through Ohio.
There is off I-75 in Ohio a mosque, so life
goes corn corn corn mosque, I wave at Islam,
which we're not getting along with
on account of the Towers as I pass.
Then Ohio goes corn corn corn
billboard, goodbye, Islam. You never forget
how to be from Michigan when you're from Michigan.
It's like riding a bike of ice and fly-fishing.
The Upper Peninsula is a spare state
in case Michigan goes flat. I live now
in Virginia, which has no backup plan
but is named the same as my mother,
I live in my mother again, which is creepy
but so is what the skin under my chin is doing,
suddenly there's a pouch like marsupials
are needed. The state joy is spring.
"Osiris, we beseech thee, rise and give us baseball"
is how we might sound were we Egyptian in April,
when February hasn't ended. February

is thirteen months long in Michigan.
We are a people who by February
want to kill the sky for being so gray
and angry at us. "What did we do?"
is the state motto. There's a day in May
when we're all tumblers, gymnastics
is everywhere, and daffodils are asked
by young men to be their wives. When a man elopes
with a daffodil, you know where he's from.
In this way I have given you a primer.
Let us all be from somewhere.
Let us tell each other everything we can.

ACKNOWLEDGMENTS

I'd like to thank the editors, copyeditors, secretaries, jockeys, key-grips, illusionists, soothsayers, and welders of the following publications: *American Poetry Review, Believer, Black Warrior Review, Diode, DMQ Review, Field, Forklift, Georgia Review, Gettysburg Review, Green Mountains Review, Gulf Coast, Iowa Review, Iron Horse Literary Review, Kenyon Review, Los Angeles Review, Many Mountains Moving, Massachusetts Review, Mid-American Review, Mississippi Review, Missouri Review, New England Review, Parthenon West, Ploughshares, Poetry Daily, Poetry Northwest, Smartish Pace, Southern Review, Stride Magazine*, and *Verse Daily*.

"a history of origami" and "A primer" first appeared in the *New Yorker*.

"In the loop," "Learning to swim," and "A shopkeeper's story" first appeared in *Poetry*.

"Methodical" was reprinted in *The Pushcart Prize XXXIII*.

"Epithalamium" was reprinted in *The Pushcart Prize XXXIV*.

Many thanks to Tom Gardner, Ada Limón, and Matthew Siegel for reading this manuscript.

And I'd like to express my gratitude to the John Simon Guggenheim Foundation and the National Endowment for the Arts. For the money, certainly, but o so more so the belief.